I0816951

SYMBOLS OF THE USA!

THE STAR-SPANGLED BANNER

by Julie Murray

Cody Koala

An Imprint of Pop!

popbooksonline.com

Hello! My name is Cody Koala

This book is filled with videos, puzzles, games, and more! Scan the QR codes* while you read, or visit the website below to make this book pop.

popbooksonline.com/SSB

*Scanning QR codes requires a web-enabled smart device with a QR code reader app and a camera.

abdobooks.com

Published by Pop!, a division of ABDO, PO Box 398166, Minneapolis, Minnesota 55439.

Printed in the United States of America, North Mankato, Minnesota.

082025
012026

THIS BOOK CONTAINS RECYCLED MATERIALS

Cover Photo: Shutterstock Images
Interior Photos: Alamy Stock Photo; Getty Images; Shutterstock Images
Editors: Elizabeth Andrews and Grace Hansen
Series Designer: Victoria Bates

Library of Congress Control Number: 2025941211

Publisher's Cataloging-in-Publication Data
Names: Murray, Julie, author.
Title: The Star-Spangled Banner / by Julie Murray
Description: Minneapolis, Minnesota : Pop!, 2026 | Series: Symbols of the USA! | Includes online resources and index
Identifiers: ISBN 9781098248659 (lib. bdg.) | ISBN 9781098249175 (ebook)
Subjects: LCSH: Star-spangled banner (Song); arranged--Juvenile literature. | National songs--Juvenile literature. | National anthems--Juvenile literature. | United States--History--War of 1812--Juvenile literature. | Signs and symbols--United States--Juvenile literature.
Classification: DDC 782.42159--dc23

Table of Contents

Chapter 1

The Star-Spangled Banner

"The Star-Spangled Banner" is one of the most important songs in United States history. Most people recognize it from its first five words, "O say can you see...."

The Star Spangled Banner
Francis Scott Key
May 15, '98
Taber.
Watch a video here!

Chapter 2

Inspiration

The song was **inspired** by a US flag that flew over **Fort** McHenry in Baltimore, Maryland. Great Britain attacked the fort on September 13, 1814. This happened during the War of 1812.

Learn more here!

Francis Scott Key was an American **lawyer** and poet. He was on a ship and saw the attack on Fort McHenry.

The next morning, Key saw that the flag was still flying. The United States kept control of the fort! It made him want to write a poem.

Chapter 3

From Poem to Song

The poem Francis Scott Key wrote was called "Defence of **Fort** McHenry." It was later renamed "The Star-Spangled Banner."

The flag from Fort McHenry can be seen in Washington D.C. It is at the Smithsonian's National Museum of American History.

Explore links here!

The poem was soon turned into a song. It was popular in the 1800s. It became the **official anthem** of the US Navy in 1889.

Chapter 4

The National Anthem

On March 3, 1931, President Herbert Hoover made "The Star-Spangled Banner" the **official** national **anthem** of the United States. It is played at military and sports events and other gatherings.

"The Star-Spangled Banner" has four verses. Usually, only the first verse is sung.

Complete an activity here!

To show patriotism,
people stand and face the
flag while the song is played.

Some people put their hand over their heart.

Patriotism is love and respect for one's country.

The stars of the flag stand for the 50 states in the United States. Over time, more stars were added to the flag as more states joined the country.

The stripes on the flag stand for the 13 original British **colonies** that won their freedom and started the United States.

"The Star-Spangled Banner" stands for **resilience** and **unity** in the United States. It brings great **pride** to the American people.

Making Connections

Text-to-Self

Have you ever been at an event where "The Star-Spangled Banner" was played? How did it make you feel?

Text-to-Text

Have you read any other books about the US flag and "The Star-Spangled Banner"? What did you learn?

Text-to-World

The song was inspired by the War of 1812. Have you heard of any other wars? What do you know about them?

Glossary

anthem – a song of praise and patriotism.

colony – a place where a group of people come to settle that is controlled by their home country.

fort – a strong building used during battles for protection and defense.

lawyer – one whose job is to help people with legal matters and represent them in court.

official – approved by an authority; formal and public.

pride – a sense of personal value that comes from what one has or can do.

resilience – the ability to withstand and survive difficulties.

unity – the condition of acting as one.

Index

Online Resources

popbooksonline.com

Thanks for reading this Cody Koala book!

This book is filled with videos, puzzles, games, and more! Scan the QR codes* while you read, or visit the website below to make this book pop.

popbooksonline.com/SSB

*Scanning QR codes requires a web-enabled smart device with a QR code reader app and a camera.